D1741166

STUMBLE INTO
YOUR OWN
BOOKKEEPING
BUSINESS

DAWN HAMMOND

MIDAS PUBLISHING
Part of Hammond & Co
www.hammondandco.co.uk

ISBN: 978-1-291-61283-7

HOW TO USE THIS BOOK

It sounds a little daft telling someone how to read a book, don't you think? But this book is written in two halves. The first telling a little about me and how I managed to get my business up and running. The second part telling you what you should do to get your business up and running.

Feel free to read whichever half first or feel free to ignore one half completely.

CONTENTS

INTRODUCTION

My name is Dawn Hammond, I own Hammond & Co. and Beans Accounting. Both my business run side by side and they're both very successful. Between them I have 26 regional offices operated by independent practice managers by the way of franchises.

I started from a small desk in the corner of my bedroom and built the business client by client until it was big enough to branch out to other areas.

I started off with no knowledge, a dead end part-time job that held no prospects and an idea that I wanted to be a bookkeeper. Now almost ten years later I'm the owner of Hammond & Co. an accounting practice that offers its services to nationwide clients and the Director of Beans Accounting, an accounting and bookkeeping practice that has 26 regional operators throughout the UK.

If I can start from scratch, from less than £50 in the bank, with no knowledge of bookkeeping or accounting and with the idea that I knew what I wanted to do but didn't know how to get what I wanted, then anyone can do it.

If you have a goal and you want to achieve it, if you want to succeed then you can, No one can stop you, the only person who can limit your success is you. You've taken the first step in achieving your goal of starting a bookkeeping business by reading this book.

If, once you've read the book, you decide you don't feel like going it alone but you like the business and the financial reward that comes with this type of business, then you can always contact me and take advantage of one of my franchises!

IT'S ALWAYS GOOD TO START
AT THE BEGINNING!

I was working part-time in a shop on the outside of Leeds Market, I would stand up all day serving people as they came in to try on one of the outfits in the window. The shop sold party outfits and frilly things such as tutu's so most of the clientele consisted of showgirls who were really men that performed as drag acts or the more outlandish woman who wanted to go out in a risqué outfit.

The job itself was enjoyable, I didn't enjoy the journey to work as I had to catch a bus or train and it added around an hour and half to my mornings and the same on a night, so my day was three hours longer already. The shop was cold in winter and due to its location was noisy due to the main road and the traffic.

My boss, who I thought was my friend back then, asked her friend if she wanted to work in the shop so that we could run it between us. She said yes and we worked together and had a good laugh at the same time. I'd been there around a year longer than her friend but one day I came in and I was told that she'd been made shop manager. I was a little set back, but I wished her good luck and got on with the days' work.

That night on the bus home I couldn't get it out of my mind, I'd shown her friend how to do almost everything in the shop and I hadn't even been asked about the position. It was really getting to me and I decided right there that the first thing in the morning I was going to ask her why she was asked and not me and also why she hadn't told me until after she'd been made manager.

When I got to work the next day I asked her why she'd not told me about it and she told me to ask my boss. I asked and my boss turned really nasty towards me, I was on the verge of crying but didn't give them the satisfaction of letting either of them see me upset. From that moment on things went sour, everything I did they found a problem with, even though I'd done the same thing in the past without complaint and sometimes with compliments. I know it was because I'd opened my mouth that things went downhill and to this day I have no idea as to the real reason why they wanted me to leave the shop. I didn't know anything about cash flow or balance sheets back then, but I'm guessing they had to make cut backs due to a cash flow problem and I was the one they'd picked to save them money, after all, my boss wouldn't want to upset her friend would she?

It got to the point where I couldn't even go into the shop without feeling sick so I called it a day and didn't go back, due to how I'd been treated I could have taken it further and because it was such a small business it would have had a catastrophic effect on their profit, but I didn't think they were worth the hassle or effort and I knew that they'd never grow and would always be a little shop on the edge of a market.

I walked by the shop on my way to Harvey Nichols last year and glanced in, I saw my ex-friend still working there in the small shop on the edge of Leeds market. It was cold that day so I knew the shop would feel cold too and it was my other half "Darren" who stopped me walking in to say thanks for the push, I was dressed in my usual designer stuff so a "Pretty Woman" moment went through my head. If I'm honest I believe I owe them a debt of gratitude because I wouldn't have such a successful business if they hadn't have stabbed me in the back, and who knows, it could have been me in that shop on a cold day whilst another rich woman walked by looking in!

LETS' GET EDUCATED!

So back to then… Being pushed out of my job was a little upsetting at the time, but after a few days I felt as if a burden had been lifted from my shoulders and I started to relax. So I'd left the shop and had time at home to spend with my daughter who was then still at the local infant school, I went down to see the childminder and told her that I'd lost my job, we had a cup of tea and a chat and I told her I'd be looking after Abbie-Leigh full time from now on, she was fine with it and we've been great friends ever since. Although she keeps saying she's dropping her accounts off but never gets around to it!

I decided that I wanted to learn bookkeeping so I got on the internet to look at courses, I'd worked out that I couldn't spend too much on a course as I'd only got £50 spare and if I didn't do something soon that £50 would be gone.

I found a correspondence course that suited me and offered all the basic information I needed, enough to give me the knowledge to start on my own. I thought if I did the course I could get a client or two and learn as I earn, I could tell the client I was new and reduce their fees so at least I could earn a little but at the same time use them to practice on as I learned.

This all happened in my head within seconds, it was my epiphany moment, the moment the lights went on.. But that elated feeling didn't last long when I scrolled down to the price at the bottom of the website… £360, Oh no, I'm £310 short, the postage on the item was £25, that was half my budget just on postage alone… I felt like my dreams were taken away from me, I had visions of becoming a stay at home single mum living on the dole and looking forward to benefit day.

I was just about to close the page on the website and I saw a small box at the bottom that read "Instalments", I clicked on the link and it took me to another page. The page said that I could pay for it at only £30 per month over 12 months. I clicked the terms and it said that I could pay a deposit today of £30 and then pay another £360 over the next year.

I signed up on the spot, put in my debit card details hoping that the training company would take the money quickly so that I could get my first part and get started. I printed out the receipt and put the training providers web site in my favourites, I then re-read what the course offered and started making notes.

The next few days passed really slowly, I remember feeling really depressed when the postman came and didn't have my course. Almost a week had gone by and there was a knock at the door, I answered and it was the postman with a big white parcel, he asked for my name, which he knew but asked anyway, I then signed for the parcel, took it from him, said goodbye and closed the door.

I opened my course and went through everything; it was the first months' work plus a load of other stuff that I still haven't used to this day such as a jotter, pencil and key ring with the training companies name on.

I did the first month's course in less than a week and sent back my assignments; I posted it off rather than email it because I'd nothing to do now for another month until the next part came so I wasn't bothered about rushing it. Within the week the assignment came back to me marked and a covering letter from my tutor. The letter mentioned that I should email from now on to save time and expense, but it also pointed out my assignment score and tutor feedback. The score was 100% and the feedback said "Well dine Dawn on your first assignment, keep up the great work".. and no, I haven't made a spelling mistake, it really did say "Well *dine* Dawn".

To my surprise the very next day the second part of the course turned up, month two. I telephoned the company and told them that I wasn't expecting it as I was only in the first month and after giving the woman my student number she informed me that the next part of the course is sent out automatically once the previous part is completed and signed off as "passed" with the personal tutor. The miracles of the internet age!

This meant that if I got my finger out, used the email instead of normal snail mail, I could get things done quicker and it gave me longer to find the money because at this rate I could finish the course before I've paid the full amount. I'd be able to earn money to actually pay for the course, a win-win situation for me.

I just had to find a couple of customers who didn't mind that I didn't know too much, but looking at my first assignment feedback I knew it wouldn't be long before I'd be in a position to charge a good amount and I knew I could learn what was needed as I went along. I liked this bookkeeping lark and I knew it was going to be a career for me from here on… Now all I needed was a willing test customer who'd forgive me if I messed things up.

Another month passed me by and I used what spare time I had while Abbie-Leigh was at school to learn as much as I could. As well as having my coursework in my hand at every opportunity, I also spent time on the internet looking at how other bookkeeping businesses had started up, but most importantly, what they were charging. I made around 50 phone calls to every bookkeeping business I could find to enquire about the price they charged.

With an average price structure in mind I thought it would be time to ask all my family if they knew anyone with a business, I was happy to take on anyone and offer them cut price bookkeeping just so I could raise the monthly course fees needed to complete the course. I went around all my family and told them I was now bookkeeping and I'd offer their friends a family discount if they used me.

Another month went by and I was starting to think that I'd never get my first "test" client, I needed to get some hands on experience to gain the knowledge I needed, but most importantly I needed the money, even if it was only going to be around a fiver an hour. I thought about the local newspaper and decide to phone them so I drafted out what I thought was the perfect advert and picked the phone up. Less than one minute into the call I remember saying very loudly *"How much?"* and then putting the phone down.

The only other option was a small advertiser that I'd seen in the local shops, a free paper that contained lots of different businesses. I thought that if small businesses are in it then it must work for them, also, I was sure that everyone in the advertiser would see me and use me. I gave them a call and before I knew it I'd placed my advert for a quarter of the cost of the last newspaper and they'd even said they'd print my logo and put me in a box. Me!, in an advertising box with a professional logo at the side of my name, it felt real all of a sudden and I made sure my mobile phone was turned up so I could hear it when they eventually started to phone me and I made sure I carried a pen and paper in my pocket just in case I was called when I was picking my daughter up from school.

RUNNING OUT OF TIME

As I sat reading my coursework and working on my course I kept looking at my mobile phone. The advert had been in the advertiser for the last week and I was yet to get an inquiry. I looked at my phone and checked I had a good signal, I re-read the advert and checked my number was correct, the signal was on four bars and the number in the advert was correct.

Not a single enquiry had come forward, not even another bookkeeper trying to find out what I was charging. I didn't understand it, talk about disheartened, upset wasn't the word, I had no idea what I was going to do now and I didn't know about advertising and I didn't have a clue how I could get customers.

The next day the man from the advertiser phoned me, *"would you like to re book your advert for next week Miss Hammond?"* he asked, *"No thank you, I haven't had a single call"* I replied. He came back with *"you have to advertise around nine times before the customer trusts you"*, *"you didn't say that when I gave you the money"* I said, and then I hung up. I know it wasn't the advertising mans' fault that the potential customers didn't phone me, but at that point in time it was totally his fault and it was his fault that I went out to the newsagent and spent £2 that I couldn't afford on a job paper.

I came in from the shop, put the kettle on and put the paper next to my cup. I made a cup of tea, and went to sit down to read the paper and see if I could get a job similar to what I knew how to do, a job in retail was now my destiny, bookkeeping was a good idea at the time and my own business seemed a fantastic idea, but who was I kidding? I wasn't any sort of businesswoman, let alone one that does number crunching for other successful businesses, who was I fooling?

I couldn't stand to open the job paper, simply buying it had upset me and filled me with disappointment, I was a quitter and I was starting to regret signing up for the bookkeeping course because I had to pay for it now and it wasn't even going to be put to use.

I took a mouthful of tea and started to look through the paper, I started looking for the retail section but before that I noticed the accounting section, I had a skim through and saw around sixteen jobs on offer. I thought for a moment and wondered if I could get a job as a trainee, I sat there for a minute or so and then it hit me. If sixteen companies wanted accountants then that meant that there was a demand for my services and I was quitting too early.

I picked up the advertiser again, the one that I was in but didn't work for me, I looked at the other advertisers inside and decided to give one of them a call and ask what his response was like and if he's had any work from the paper. I dialled the first one I saw who turned out to be a plumber, when he answered I told him that I advertised in the advertiser on the same page as him and asked if he'd had anyone phone him about any work. He said *"yes, I'm a plumber and I get plenty of work"*, *"great"* I replied *"and I bet your accountants happy with the increase in work then? All those extra transactions in your books"* he then said *"I don't have an accountant"*, *"do you need one"* I said, and then came the magic words *"I could do with a bit of help in the tax return department"*, Eureka, I'd drummed up my own lead and it looked like I'd made a sale.

I went on to tell him that I was new to the industry but was willing to reduce my fee to a fiver an hour on condition he told all his mates about me and I then swore him to secrecy as to how much he was paying, I said that if he brought a friend to me as a new client I'd give his friends a special rate of only £7.50 an hour but only for the first two clients he introduced to me. He was happy with the idea and I arranged to meet him the next day to collect his paperwork and get to work.

The good mood swept over me, so long as I didn't do anything stupid at our meeting I was now in business, the good news didn't stop there, I picked up the phone and did the same again, but I started the conversation with *"Hi, I'm Dawn from Hammonds Professional Bookkeeping Services, we advertise in the same local paper, in fact you're on the same page as me, can I ask if you've had any new customers from the paper?"* that broke the ice, after letting them speak I then went in with the killer question *"Well as I mentioned, I run Hammonds Professional Bookkeeping Services and I'm offering a huge discount on bookkeeping services to businesses in our local area. I can help you with your books for only £7.50 an hour and I already do the books for other businesses in the area, I help most of them with their tax returns"* I had no idea how to do a tax return at that time and wasn't even 100% sure what one actually was, but I remember seeing a course while on the internet that claimed to show you all about them, so all being well by the time the tax returns came round, I'd be able to do them.

He said he'd be happy to give me a go at that rate and said he'd tell his friend at the site that he was working on in the morning as his friend was looking for someone to sort his books out too.

Not too bad, less than fifteen minutes on the phone and I'd got an appointment for tomorrow evening with a plumber, another the evening after with an electrician and a word of mouth referral on the cards. Not too bad to say that less than twenty minutes ago I was thinking about packing it all in and going back to work in a shop.

IS THAT A NETTO BAG OR ARE YOU JUST GLAD TO SEE ME?

The appointment was only half an hour away and I'd been unable to sleep the night before as I was rehearsing what I would say to the new client. What if he asked me something I didn't know? Which at that point in time was anything about bookkeeping, I knew enough from the course so far to be able to tell him what was put in what column and what was able to go through the books and I had almost got on top of what was a liability and what was an asset.

I had a suit type dress thing that didn't look out of place at a wedding and that's what I decided to wear. I was a little green back then and thought that people in business had to dress a certain way. Nowadays it comes natural to me and I like my designer names, but back then I had a lot less money and just hoped I looked the part.

I had a leather laptop bag that looked like a women's briefcase, so I padded it out with paper and other stuff so it looked like I was busy and took it along to the meeting.

Two minutes before I was due to arrive I knocked on the door of the plumbers house. *"Hello"* I said *"I hope I've got the right house"*, *"yes"* he replied *"the big van with Plumber written on it at the side of you on the drive sort of gives it away"* and laughed, I laughed with him only mine was more from embarrassment as I'd been to engrossed in my thoughts to even look at the large silver van as I walked passed it up the driveway.

We went inside and his wife offered me a drink, I said yes to be polite but didn't get around to drinking it due to nerves and talking about his business. After what seemed like ten minutes but was in fact almost an hour, I asked him for his paperwork and he sent his wife to what he called his office, *"go get my paperwork from the office will you Becks"* he said and she soon returned with a Netto carrier bag full of screwed up paper. At first I thought she'd emptied the office bin and was on her way to throw it in the dustbin, but she gave the bag to the plumber. He had a look inside and then passed it to me, *"here's my paperwork love, it's not in any particular order, do you think you can sort it?"* *"of course, no problem"* I replied and I stood up, I said my goodbyes, shook hands, thanked him for the tea that I didn't drink and told him I'd have it done by the end of the week. *"great stuff"* he said *"and I've told a couple of mates about you so expect a call, if you don't hear anything by the time you bring my stuff back let me know and I'll chase them up"*.

I left the house without looking back and walked home as quick as I could clutching a Netto bag full of receipts and invoices with the promise of more work to come. At last I was in business, it was only £5 an hour business, but tomorrow was £7.50 business and I knew it was going to work out for me.

NUMBER CRUNCHING

I couldn't wait to get through the door and get my teeth in to real life accounts, I spent the next two hours sorting out the ins from the outs then I put everything in the right months. I checked it all again and then put it to one side until tomorrow when my daughter had gone to school.

I'd taken Abs' to school and I came home as fast as I could to crack on with the work, I spent most of the morning inputting the figures into an accounting software program that I'd bought from eBay for £2.99 with free postage. I knew it wasn't up to much and that I'd have to buy a half decent bookkeeping package but I just couldn't afford it yet and the main thing about the eBay purchase was that it looked good in the listing and it did what it said on the cover, actually it didn't have a cover due to the price.

I printed the worksheets containing all the ins and outs out and stapled them together using a piece of red card that I'd cut into a triangle to make the stapled corner look good, it looked very legal with its red corner on, a bit like a solicitors document. I put an invoice together and worked out what he owed me and I placed all the receipts and invoices in a couple of spare "polly pockets" that I had in the house. The total for the bookkeeping and bringing everything up to date, including preparing the accounts in a lovely little stapled bundle came to £50, not much, but for my first go and my first client I was very happy, I'd have worked a day and half for that in the market shop, so I saw it as a result, plus it was my money that I'd earned from nothing so the invoice felt even sweeter than a wage slip.

I had to walk fast to pick Abs' up from school as I'd gotten carried away with my new business and I'd also forgotten that I had arranged to meet the electrician just after tea. I got my sister "Kelly" to keep an eye on her and I went to my appointment as planned. I took the plumbers accounts so that I could show the sparky what he would be getting for his £7.50 an hour.

The meeting went really well and I was surprised when he phoned his mate up halfway through the meeting and had him make an appointment with me for the following night. I waited for his Netto bag but was relieved to find that he had his paperwork in a folder, I was also a little deflated because it meant that I wouldn't get to spend as long on his books and less time equalled less money, but on the bright side, I was charging this bloke £2.50 an hour more and he was very happy with the layout of the plumbers accounts, Plus, he'd set up my next client and word of mouth is the best advertising you can get.

The electricians accounts were sorted the next day and the invoice was prepared as soon as I'd finished, making a total from the electricians accounts of £45. I'd made a grand total of £95 in two days doing easy work and doing something I enjoyed, the best part was that the work was repeatable and I was going to do the same for them the next time and now I'd got their books in order it was just a matter of telling them that I should sort them every month to keep their costs down.

I signed up the referral from the electrician and repeated the process, completing the work, raising the invoice and then the following week I delivered everyone their work back and handed them the invoices, all three paid cash and I came away with £145. Not much but for a new business I was over the moon.

A BACON SANDWICH PLEASE!

I had a craving for bacon and right fancied a bacon sandwich, we didn't have any in the fridge so I decided to treat myself and spend a couple of quid out of my newly labelled "petty cash" tin. A week had passed since invoicing my three new clients and I was back with my nose stuck inside a course book.

I had a walk down to the local sandwich shop and went inside, I ordered a bacon sandwich and sat on one of those tall stools next to a worktop stuck to the wall. Just above the worktop was an array of business cards stuck to the wall with a selection of sticky tape, blue tack and drawing pins. I glanced through and wondered if any of them had a bookkeeper.

"Do you get plenty of workmen in here then?" I said to the girl behind the counter, *"Oh yeh!, loads en em"* she replied. *"Would it be OK for me to pop a leaflet on the wall the next time I'm in here? I'm a professional bookkeeper that deals with tradesmen"* *"Yeh! why not, at least you asked, rest en um just stick a card up wiyart askin when the lookin at paper"* she said, in an accent that sounded like an extra from Emmerdale.

I took my sandwich and had a walk home eating it out of the bag, as I was eating it I was thinking about a leaflet and what to put on it, from what she had said it sounded like I had to keep it simple and right to the point. I got back home and powered up my computer and designed what I thought back then was the mother of all leaflets, the King of all flyers, a leaflet that would be the envy of all public relations and advertising companies.. An A5 black and white leaflet that said "Do you need an accountant / bookkeeper that understands the construction industry? – Then phone 07730 123456". I made the type big to fill the white paper and took a copy back down to the sandwich shop the same day. I placed it in the middle of the display and moved a few business cards to one side. Thanked Annie Sugden and left. Just in case you're under forty years old, Annie Sugden was the main character from Emmerdale Farm before it went all posh and dropped the "farm" bit.

I had just reached my gate when my mobile phone rang.. *"Hello, Dawn Hammond, Hammond Professional Bookkeeping Services, can I help you"*, I don't answer like that anymore, after all I was new to business and I've also dropped the "Professional Bookkeeping Services " bit of the title and gone with "& Co." since moving into accountancy. Anyway, it was a bloke in the sandwich shop who needed his books sorted out as soon as possible. I'd only just put the leaflet up and I'd had a call, my king of flyers, mother of all leaflets worked and it was still the same day.

I made an appointment to meet the new tradesman who turned out to be a plasterer, I told him it was £10 an hour, showed him a copy of the plumbers accounts which I'd now changed the name and figures and made a set of dummy accounts to show prospective clients. He gave me his paperwork and I skipped home like I'd won the lottery.

Slowly over a couple of months I completed my bookkeeping course, sat an exam and passed with 99% and a distinction. I decided not to take any more courses just yet and that I'd try to work at building my practice up. I'd only got seven clients so far and even though the work and fees were residual I couldn't rely on the small amount of money that was left at the end of the month.

I decided to visit all the cafes, sandwich shops, newsagents and fish shops in the area and put my killer flyer up. Some charged me some didn't, one bloke even said it was a quid for a week which I paid to make sure I was in every shop and café in the area, that way every sandwich eating, Mars bar munching, chip scoffing workman in the area would see my advert, they might not use me today, but tomorrow or next week when they were getting cod and chips for lunch, they would see my king of all flyers shining down on them like a heaven sent message of bookkeeping help.

SPECIALISING

I don't know why but for some reason I sort of fell into the building trade and marketed to tradesman, because my first client was a tradesman and the second, third and fourth, it just seemed natural that I should attract tradesman and specialise as the one who could sort out their books.

I'd been running a year now and during that time I'd been subjected to phrases that the course didn't cover such as C.I.S, main contractor contributions and capital repairs. So a good bit of my time was spent in the library or Waterstones reading the books on tax and accounting to get me up to speed.

I'm sure the woman in Waterstones thought I was a female plumber at times and I even went as far as buying an NVQ construction book so that I could learn the lingo.

The construction industry was great, you got what you saw with the tradesman, not too big on manners and they said what they meant. In return it allowed me to keep away from jargon I didn't understand at the time and tell them that I said it in their words which made me sound even better to them. So rather than explain to one of them that their new tool purchase had to go down as an asset and it would depreciate over time and I think we'll use the straight line method of depreciation, I simply said *"that's a decent bit of kit, I'll put it in your accounts and let you know when it's worth less"*

Because I learned about the construction industry it gave me an insight into the world of the tradesman, I knew what they were charging, what price they were quoting, what they were paying for the materials and what their bottom line was. On the odd occasion I have to get a builder out today, they'd be hard pressed to give me a high price and when I start talking to them and asking them where they're buying their materials from and that they should try such and such builders merchants to save a fiver on a tonne of gravel, they go a little quiet. A woman who knows about building.. *"is this a modern day witch?"* I can hear them thinking, and then I see them discretely looking around for a camera and hoping that Mat Alright from Rogue Traders isn't about to jump out on them, it takes a strong cup of tea and business card along with an explanation that I specialise in the accounts of builders to calm them down.

It's not just builders and tradesmen that we deal with, I'd be daft to turn down other businesses, but my rule is that I must know about the business before I take on the work. We have many clients who run hair salons and beauty salons, so that was the next thing. I spent hours learning about hair products, suppliers, acrylic nails and even solar exposure on sunbeds just so that I could be prepared to understand the clients business. My partner Darren, partner as in we're getting married, helps me with the business and has become a shareholder and director, so I suppose he's my multi-partner, has learned hair dressing and styling so that he can give advice to hair salons. He can give business advice to the stylist and if need be he could pick up the scissors and create a masterpiece. This is the sort of knowledge that sets us apart from the regular accountants who only know about numbers and tax.

Darren is also a fully qualified electrician for domestic and commercial electrics, that's because we deal with both sorts of electricians. He has an NVQ level 3 in plastering, the same in bricklaying and a BTEC in construction and surveying, so which accountant and business adviser would you choose if you were a builder?... The one behind the desk or the one who can help you rewire a house as you chat about profit and loss?

All the time and effort that has gone into learning the clients business inside out has really paid off, we have clients from every business sector on our books and we have an accountant who knows their business inside out. B&Q do the same with their retail staff, you want to know about plumbing then the plumbing retail assistant helps you chose the right part for the job, that's because he used to be a professional plumber, the same with the electrical assistant and that's why they are so successful.

We have a printer on the books, and guess what?.. Yes, we have an ex-printer who knows everything on the subject. Without specialising we would not have built the business, without offering extra and without the industry knowledge we wouldn't be able to compete with the bigger companies. We wouldn't be where we are today.

I THINK IT'S TIME TO GET HELP

I'd been running the business single handed for the past eighteen months to two tears now and I was trying to do everything myself. I knew that I'd have to eventually get someone in to help but at the moment I needed to ensure that everything was done to my standard. If I buckled under the pressure and took someone on then they might not do the job right, and that would mean complaints from happy clients and.. well it doesn't bare thinking about.

I'd had a hard time in my past with Abbie-Leighs dad, we didn't get on very well and we'd called it a day. I'd met "Darren", he was best mates with my best mates' husband and we just clicked. We've been together for seven years, we never argue, we have a difference of opinion but once he sees I'm right that's the end of it.

Darren's a true entrepreneur, when we got together he had a cleaning business, an electrical contracting business, a column in the newspaper and was a part-time police officer. Unlike my ex, Darren has always motivated me and pushed me to achieve my goals, just in case he's reading this, and he probably is, I just want to point out that I'd have done it without him anyway, but being able to talk to someone who's like-minded and knows about business tends to speed things up a little. After a long talk about my concerns for Hammond & Co and how I could cope on my own, he persuaded me to take the plunge and get help. After all, one person running a business can't go national can they? It's impossible to run a multi-office operation from the desk in the corner of the bedroom.

My first major move was to get an office, Darren had built a walk in office in the corner of the bedroom that worked fine, I could pull large mirrored doors over the office recess and it disappeared as if it was never there, but the paperwork was piling up and overtaking the house. At one point we had paperwork in the kitchen and had to cook meals around it, that's when we knew that a bigger office was needed.

I looked on the internet but couldn't find anything, the only thing I could find was serviced offices which were shared with other businesses, a sort of business centre with a receptionist at the front desk.

Unable to find a stand-alone office or shop front within my price range I decided to phone a business centre up and made an appointment to go see the layout and the office they were renting out. I went along and had a good look around, the office was quite large, big enough to fit about ten desks in, the reception was professional and for an extra charge they even answered the phone in your company name before putting the call through to me.

To cut a long story short, I took the office, rented some desks, bought a lovely plant, pictures, and sorted the office out. It looked the part but I was lost in it, just me sat at a desk working, I felt bored and lonely until eventually I decided to get an assistant to help me.

An advert was placed in the local newspaper on the Tuesday, they ran the advert on the Thursday and the phone rang all day Friday. The following Tuesday I'd set up interviews and had a list of key questions to ask the potential client. 10.30 am, the first candidate arrived, the reception phoned me, and said *"Miss Hammond, a Miss Carver to see you, should I send her up?"* very professional, *"Yes"* I replied and waited for the knock.

Knock, Knock, Knock and the door slowly opened and in walked my first candidate. *"Please, sit down"* I said and pulled a chair out for her, *"So, you're Miss Carver?, tell me why do you want to work in bookkeeping and accounts?"* and I waited for the reply, she thought a moment and said *"Well... I want to be a hair stylist but the course was full, so I was thinking.. if I do this for a year then I can go to college next year and it's something for me to do while I'm waiting",* "OK" I said, *"but it's not the best answer is it?",* *"Spose not, but do you know what it's like in the beauty industry? It's like really well hard to get into, you wunt know about hair styling been an accountant and that and you dote av any idea about hair so.., you know what I mean?"* I had to take a moment to take in what she'd just said and then said *"Yes I know what you mean, and I know everything there is to know about the hair and beauty industry, I have contacts and friends who own salons throughout Yorkshire, I could pick that phone up right now and get you a job in a salon from one of the many people that owe me a favour, but what I'd like you to do first, and this is a test, stand up and walk towards the door, open it and close it behind you.. OK?"* she looked at me, stood up, walked to the door and just before closing it she turned around and said *"you know that thing you said about hair?.. well whatever"* then SLAM!

The kettle went on followed by a twenty minute relax with my feet on the desk looking out of the window towards the building site over the road, I thought to myself *"I wonder if any of them are self-employed",* I think that every time I see someone in a work van or carrying tools, I really need to stop it and learn to walk by without thinking about building my business. My phone rang and for a moment I'd forgotten all about the business as I'd been trying to figure out what they were building over the road, *"A Mrs Hunter to see you Miss Hammond, should I send her up?",* *"Yes please"* and I sat up, shuffled some papers and brushed myself down.

The knock on the door came in less than a minute of me putting the phone down and I invited her in. In walked a strict looking woman with her grey hair in a bun, grey clothes, brown shoes and a serious look on her face. She looked like a nanny or governess and she placed a typed out CV in front of me before sitting down. I introduced myself and then asked the question *"So why do you want to be a bookkeeper?"* she paused for a moment and *replied "if you look at my CV you'll see everything you need to know about me"* oooh!, right to the point I thought, *"I'm not one for CV's so please tell me"* I pushed the CV towards her and waited for her reply. *"Everything you need to know, qualifications, references and such can be found on this"* and she pushed it back to my side of the desk, *"Well I'd like you to tell me please"* and I pushed it back, *"It's all on here"* as she slid it back to me, I could see a game of paper tennis pursuing if I didn't change tactics so I said *"well let's pretend I can't read, tell me in your own words", "can't you"* she said, *"can't I what?" "can't you read?"* she asked, *"It's just a saying"* I said *"Just pretend I can't read and tell me about you, I want to get to know you better, after all, we may be working together"*… *"No, I don't do that sort of thing, I like to stick to the rules"* she replied, *"What rules"* I wanted to know what these rules were, who had written them and why hadn't I seen the book during my hours of pretend buying in Waterstones. *"The rules of interviewing, you must be factual and as such I've given you my CV which contains all the relevant information on me"* and she pushed the stapled pieces of paper which were already on my side of the desk nearer to me.

"OK, I'll read it" I said *"but it may take some time, so I'll do it at home tonight"* she didn't look amused, she had a scowl on her face like a teacher who didn't like children, she tutted, stood up and walked towards the door. I waited to see if she said anything but she walked out and I never saw her again. Although, I do believe I've seen her hair bun, but it had parted company with her and it was on another woman's head in Costa.

The interviewing was going really well, both of the candidates so far were awful, I now knew how Simon Cowell felt when he held an audition in Manchester, I only had two more people to see and the next one wasn't for over an hour thanks to Nanny McPhee walking off.

Back to the building site and the chair near the window, two cups of Earl Grey and half an hour of eBay later the phone rang. *"Miss Hammond, I have a huge arse to see you"* said the woman on the other end, *"Pardon"* did I hear that correctly or had I become so bored I was imagining things, *"a Mr Hugh Jarse would like to see you, should I send him up?"* it was really hard to say yes without laughing but I told her to send him up. I ran to the desk, sat behind it and picked up a pen so that I could pretend to be writing. Knock, Knock.. *"Come in"*, *"Hello I'm Mr Jarse"* said Darren, *"Pretending to write something down are you"* he said, well at least it cheered me up.

I think it was around another fifteen minutes before the phone rang, I did the same as before and said to send them up and Darren left just as they were getting there. Things went from bad to worse, this one thought he was vampire, he was dressed in black from head to toe and had pierced lips, ears and eyebrows and even had what appeared to be black lipstick.

The next one was from the job centre and had come along so that she could say she'd actually done something this week and put it on her job seekers record. How do I know this? She told me, she said she didn't want the job but she's happy to come along as it helps with the job seekers record. My god, what was this world coming to, I had a job on offer, I wanted to pay someone to help me out and I couldn't even attract a normal person, I'd had enough today, I was going home for a hot bath, a nice home cooked tea and a really good moan.

BUILD ME AN OFFICE THEN!

I spent a full week in a large office in the middle of a city looking out of the window trying to figure out what they were building over the road. I watched lorries dumping rubble and workmen leaning against shovels watching young girls walk by without taking their eyes off them. I honestly think that builders on building sites are the missing link between humans and barn owls, and the way those builders could twist their necks all the way around when a girl walked passed them proves this fact beyond all reasonable doubt.

By the end of the week I'd had enough and couldn't wait to get home and do nothing all weekend, what had turned out to be my great plan for world domination had done nothing for me apart from lumber me with a big office and no staff.

It got to one o'clock on Friday and I went home. When I got home Darren was in his work shed place, a brick built outhouse with electrics in it that he kept his tools in and he'd used it to do his paperwork in there out of the way and keep his business separate from the house. I took him a pot of tea out and told him how I felt.

"You're not in a contract, so leave" he said, *"Leave my big office when I've just got there"* I shouted, I actually thought it was a god idea as soon as he said it but held the pretence and replied *"I've worked hard to get that office, I intend to staff it and build the business, I started with nothing you know"* and I went into the house secretly smiling, I just had to keep up the mood for the next hour and then decide to hand my notice in on Monday and go back to the home office, this way I knew Darren would think he'd persuaded me and I'd listened to him, a win-win situation in a relationship.

He came in and said *"Look, I think you should work from home again for now, then when you get someone to help you should get another office and take it from there"* I waited because I knew something else was coming *"Or.."* he said *"you could be virtual, have the people who work for you do it from their home office via the internet, everyone's doing it nowadays"* he was on to something but the hour wasn't up yet and a knew that it had to be at least a full hour otherwise he'd know he was right. *"I'm not sure"* I said *"I can't talk on the internet via one of those webcams and have the bed behind me, and there's always the chance that you'll walk passed with your arse out, I'd still need an office"* that should do it I thought, I'm sort of going along with it but I'm not quite there yet. *"Well that's my idea anyway, it's up to you"* he said, whoops!, I might lose this cunning plan after all, I need to claw it back, *"Well build me an office then!"* I've no idea where that actually came from, it just spilled out of my mouth, like I'm going to get an office built, I think I'd been watching too many design programs on TV. *"Right then, I will"* he said and he went outside.

Abbie-Leigh had gone to her dads in Newcastle for the week so we'd decided at the beginning of the week that come Saturday we'd go out and have a nice night in a local cosy pub with a couple of friends, but the weekend got changed into a B&Q and Ikea weekend, Darren extended the garden shed, by extension I mean he doubled it in size, he moved all his tools and work stuff out of the outhouse and converted the outhouse into a small office.

It had a massive desk, filing cabinet, shelves, cupboards, carpet, complete electrical overhaul with sockets and spot lights, telephone, internet and computer, it even had a coffee machine in it for any clients who might visit. And on Sunday night he gave me the key on a Hammond & Co key ring, he'd built me an office and I loved it.

On Monday I went into my large open plan office in the city centre and told them I was leaving, we came to an agreement which allowed me to use an office there whenever I needed one for interviews or meetings as well as use them for document storage, plus it's good to have a big office on hand. I had to pay the following months' rent in full, but so what, I was going to build my empire a different way.

THE TOILET INSPECTION

Last week I'd placed an advert with the job centre and it attracted the wrong sort of candidate, I need to place it online, that way I would attract people who knew how to use a computer, after all if I was going to do the business virtually then I needed people who knew how to do virtual things.

I came across a website that would let you post a job for free and then they'd send the job to people who had signed up with them to received email notifications. After filling the online form in and then writing the job advert, I chose West Yorkshire in the little drop down box and pressed send. I folded the laptop down and went to get a brew. I gave it about twenty minutes then thought I'd have a look and see if anyone had viewed my advert and I couldn't believe what I saw, I'd already had five emails. I opened them up and deleted the two that had their CV attached as I'd said no CV's and if they couldn't read a simple seven line advert then how would they cope with numbers?

By the end of the night I'd received eighteen replies to my little advert. The following day I emailed them all back thanking them for their interest and that I'd be in touch soon. The good ones were emailed that afternoon and I asked to meet the first one the next day at their house. I could have asked them to come into the office but I wanted to see how they lived, if they lived in a squaller or the house was dirty then there was no way I was going to let them do any of my accounting, after all, if they can't look after their own property when they've paid for it then what would they be like with someone else's? It might sound a little crude or you may think I'm being a bigot, but that's my standard and it's the standard I have for my business.

I arrived at her house ten minutes early, again this is a ploy that I've used quite a few times in business. By arriving early and putting them on the spot I hope to catch them last minute vacuuming or swearing at the kids, I like to know that they keep a tight ship even when a visitor isn't coming.

I knocked on the door and a nice lady answered, *"Hello, I'm Dawn Hammond"* I said, *"Come in"* she replied and I walked in and followed her through to the sitting room. *"Nice to meet you"* I said as I discretely carried out an SAS like reconnaissance around her house by only moving my eyes, managing to face her every time she spoke to me. All looked well so far and I liked what she said, I had a good feeling about her but she had to pass the toilet test. *"All this tea has made me need the loo, do you mind if I pop to the little girls room"* I said and I waited for the excuse to follow.. *"Not at all, it's upstairs and right at the top of the steps, you can't miss it"*, so far so good, I was on my way to look down her toilet, a clean bowl gives a real insight into a persons housekeeping and if she passed the toilet test then we would be on to stage two.

Excellent, not a tank track in site, a clean bowl and thick strong toilet roll, just the sort of person that would do well at Hammonds Professional Bookkeeping Services. Now all I need to do was find out if she could actually do any bookkeeping, although I knew that having passed all the tests so far, accounting and bookkeeping were way down the list of qualifications needed to work for me and I wasn't going to let something so trivial as not knowing what she was doing stop me from giving her the job.

I walked downstairs and sat back down *"So, about your qualifications, what do you know about accounting and bookkeeping"*, she stood up and walked to the dining table in the corner of the room and handed me an envelope. *"It's not a CV is it, I don't like to play tennis"* I said *"No"* she replied *"it's my bookkeeping and accounting certificates, what do you mean by tennis?"... "I'll tell you next week when we're having a cuppa"* and I stood up, picked up my handbag and moved towards the door. *"Oh, do you need to come again next week?"* she asked.. *"No, I'd like to offer you the job and I thought we'd do all the paperwork and P45 stuff over a cup of tea at my place next Monday... I'll put it in a letter and make it official"*

She thanked me and became the first person who worked for me, She was also the first person to run an independent office when the opportunity arose and she went on to be the first person to run our North Yorkshire office.

WWW.MYBUSINESS.COM

Over the next six months I kept sending work over to Jane's house so that she could crack on with it, I kept her knee deep in paperwork while I went to meetings with clients and built the business. I came out of meetings and got on with the accounts right away and between us we knocked off a good few thousand receipts and invoices every week. We used a webcam to speak to each other as we worked and as well as me popping to her house with paperwork she would come over to my "Dazbuild" office and drop stuff off, pick things up she needed and take advantage of the coffee machine. I collated everything together once it was done and bundled it into a lovely professional looking report, I printed out the invoice and posted or returned everything back to the client, a swift operation from start to finish and everything was going great.

About now in any book or story, especially when the storyteller has just said *"things were going great"* a terrible curse unfolds followed by a downturn in luck where the author is besieged by some unknown trouble that knocks them on their arse. Well that didn't happen.. things were actually going good.

The clients were happy, I was happy and my employee was happy, I just needed to build the client base more. I didn't have a website at this point in my business, well I did, but it was crap, the website was "www.hammondsbookkeeping.co.uk" and it was grey, seriously it was grey. I'd built it when I wasn't very good at marketing and all I knew was that I needed an online presence to look serious from the outside. I now wanted to build the business and expand, one way to expand was to offer my services outside of the area and for that I needed to send potential clients to a website that was informative and would allow them to buy from it. It's called ecommerce but at that time in my business I didn't know anything about it.

I turned my attention to my website and how I could improve it from its dull grey look to something modern, also I didn't know how to put a website together so I had to learn the basics. Luckily Darrens' brother did that sort of thing so we knew that if we got stuck he'd help out, he built Darrens for his electrical company and it was a cracking site when he'd finished.

I thought that the best people to ask what they'd like to see on a website would be the clients, so I put together a questionnaire and sent it out to them. After around two weeks I think I'd received three replies so I sent the questionnaire again but this time I said that if they took part in my survey they 'd receive a 10% discount on their next accounts. As if by magic every single client returned the completed questionnaire but these were clients I already had, I needed to know how to attract more clients and once they got to the website get them to buy, my next plan would see Darren on the streets with a clip board asking people who looked like they owned businesses loads of questions.

"How the hell do I know what a business person looks like?" said Darren as I ushered him to the top end of Wakefield city centre. *"Use your common sense and just do it"* I shouted as he was walking away with his clip board *"and don't stop any scruffy people who don't look like business people"* I shouted as he walked away sticking two fingers up at me.

I honestly think that if the weather hadn't have turned nasty and the heavens open up, he would have done more than the five hours asking questions than he actually did bless him. But, I got an insight into the mind of the locals and the people who ran businesses in my area and found it.. well,.. pretty boring! One thing I found out was that grey wasn't the best colour to choose, most liked black, for some reason they said black looked expensive, which is odd because thinking back to the apprentice vampire that turned up for an interview that day, he didn't look expensive in any way. But who am I to ignore a survey, black it was then, and with the other information from the surveys I had enough info to get the new website sorted.

One of the main problems that came out during the survey was the bookkeeping, the name Hammonds Professional Bookkeeping Services didn't roll off the tongue, neither did it drum up aspirations of modernism, it was boring and made it look like all we did was bookkeeping when we had been accounting for ages.

I checked out the name "Hammond & Co" and found that the only other company with the same name was down south, of course since my Hammond & Co was born quite a few have sprung up since. Hammond & Co didn't say bookkeepers and it rolled off the tongue quite nicely.

Darrens' brother Neil managed to get me the domain name "hammondandco.co.uk" and after building the site and changing all the stationary we re-launched as Hammond & Co.

Now all I needed to do was branch out and take over England.. I wondered if Waterstones had a book on it!

THE WHEELBARROW

I received a phone call from a softly spoken bloke with a broad Yorkshire accent regarding his accounts. He had been unable to get an accountant to look at his books as he claimed they were in a bit of state. *"How bad can they be"* I asked him over the phone, *"Well love, I've tried to get em in order but I'm just no good at that sort o'thing and this last accountant I spoke to more or less told us that he want interested"*, *"OK, bring them in, do you know where we are"* I said, *"I love a doo, I'll be round this aft"*

I put the phone down and got back on with my work. Later that afternoon there was a knock at the office door, I answered it and stood before me was a well-built gentleman dressed like the typical builder, a high visability vest that was dirty, jeans covered in plaster, dust and mastic, and rigger boots that had seen better days. *"Hello"* I said, *"you must be the builder with account problems, come in"* I put my hand out to shake his and he followed me in.

"Sit down, can I get you a brew?" I asked, *"are you sure?, I'm a bit mucky love"*, said the builder, *"no problem, it'll clean, so what can I do for you?"* he went on to tell me that the last two accountants had looked at him as if he was stupid when he took his accounts into their office and asked if they could sort them, he told me that the last one even asked him to leave. *"Well you won't find snobbery here"* I said, *"I can tell that love coz you shook mi mucky hand and I'm sat down"*

"So, about these accounts that you're having problems getting sorted, have you got them with you?" he gave it a couple of seconds and then said *"I have love yes, but like I said, they're in a bit of a state, but they're all there, I've got them in the van"*, *"well you go get them and I'll get the kettle on, when you get*

back we'll get the paperwork in order and I'll welcome you to Hammond and Co, how many sugars in your tea?", "two love" and he walked out of the office.

Almost ten minutes had past and I'd made a brew, sugared it and popped it at the end of my desk for him. Then he returned but as he did he shouted *"can you give me a hand love?"* I rushed over to hold the door open so that he could squeeze a large builders wheelbarrow in through the door. After a bit of a squeeze he got it through and pushed it up to my desk leaving a bit of a wheel mark on the carpet, *"here you go love",* I looked in the wheelbarrow and saw an array of papers, some of them were torn some were crumpled up and looked like someone had attempted to iron them out, some had teacup rings on them and some were really dirty, they all had the same thing in common.. They were all held down by a large house brick.

"So can you sort them?" he asked, *"Yes, leave it with us"* we sat down and completed the usual instruction forms, he signed and I told him that I'd speak to him when we had made a dent in the pile, *"I'll give you a ring when you can come and pick the wheelbarrow up"*

It took a bit of doing and it was a two man job, but the ins and outs soon became crisp clean management reports and the receipts and invoices were filed in a couple of Hammond & Co premier client ring binders.

I gave him a ring three days later to arrange collection of the wheelbarrow that we'd been working around since he brought it in and he popped into the office the same afternoon.

"Hello Dawn love, how'd you get on?" he asked *"not too bad"* I replied *"your accounts are there"* I pointed to the wheelbarrow in the corner as I'd placed the accounts in the wheelbarrow all smart and I'd had one of the girls wrap the house brick in brown

parcel paper and stick a label on the brick which read "PAPER WEIGHT". Over the moon doesn't tell you how he felt, I was praised for doing something I love doing and he paid in cash, he's been a loyal customer ever since and we've had a few referrals from him. He no longer brings the wheel barrow in to the office as we're on top of things and like every other client we contact them to remind them that they need to bring their books up to date, but he's known affectionately in the office as the wheelbarrow man!

BEANS ACCOUNTING

I wanted to build a brand that would become a legacy to be left to my daughters, plus I had just had the good news that Daz and I were expecting a baby, we'd been trying for a while and it looked like he was the problem, after all. I'd already had a child so everything worked at my side of the factory. A sperm test and a visit to the special cubicle was booked and the day came so off he popped. The very next day after the test it turned out that I was pregnant and the jolly boys outing wasn't actually needed, but that's probably going in his book so I won't steal his thunder!

So I wanted to build a legacy, a successful brand to hand over to Abbie-Leigh and Poppy, Poppy's not born in the story yet and we still don't know we're having a girl for another seventeen weeks. Hammond & Co was a great brand, we designed new cards, a new logo and changed everything to look the part. It was a prestigious brand if I might say so myself.

The only problem was that we attracted older companies and businesses, this was fantastic because the type of businesses we were doing business with were established and "old school tie" types, but I was missing out on the new blood, the new starters, the younger clients who wanted a "no tie" approach with glass tables rather than oak desks, chrome instead of brass and high fives instead of masonic handshakes, Hammond & Co appeared to the outside to be a traditional firm.

I thought about it and didn't know what to do to attract the younger client, then I saw a cartoon in one of my accounting books that showed a man counting coffee beans and the caption said "When you said you were a bean counter, I thought you meant you were an accountant", it just clicked, I'll call my new company "Beans Accounting"

Beans Accounting was born and incorporated. I now had to decide what would be the best approach to attract all these new clients to the new snazzy brand.

I sat on my hands for a few weeks mainly due to Hammond & Co. being demanding and I got my head down and ran my business. I'd set on another two people by this time who also worked at home in their home office and spend their time between my office and theirs. We had daily talks before starting work via the internet conference software we had and I ensured they all came to the office every Friday morning to pick up their wage notes and have a face to face meeting, although it always turned out to be more of a chat about Eastenders the night before.

Then out of the blue Janes' husband Robert had been offered a job in Harrogate. I didn't see it as a problem and we thought she'd still do the same work but she wouldn't visit as much and I could pop over to hers with paperwork, it would just add an hour to the journey, also, she could pop over to the office only for important things to keep the travel down and do everything else over the phone or internet.

After a couple of weeks of nightmare logistics and travelling backwards and forwards from Wakefield to Harrogate, she decided that it was too much so we parted but remained great mates. I was a little upset because she was great to work with but although it was only a fifty minute drive it took too much time out of a working day for both of us and neither of us could afford to lose the time.

Jane had been in Harrogate now for almost four months and we stayed in touch, she enquired as to how the business was doing and I kept her up to date with the gossip. I then received an enquiry from a potential client in Harrogate, a builder who had just gone self-employed and wanted us to sort out his registration and tax affairs.

I popped over to see him the following day and phoned Jane to say that I was in the area and she should get the kettle on. All went well with the new client and I popped to Janes for a cup of Earl Grey.

While I was sat at her kitchen table I told her that the next time I pop over to return the clients paperwork I'll pop in for another brew, she knew it would be the same week as she's been working to my timescale for the past eighteen months but I told her that since she'd left I'd had to do more of the work and I hadn't got a replacement for her and that we were all doing extra until I could, so it wasn't going to be the same week turnaround on this new client.

I'd have to find the time to pop back out with the completed paperwork because I'd have to explain what the reports were and what I'd done for the money and that wasn't going to be this week simply because there wasn't enough hours in the week.

"I could always leave it for you to do, then when it's done you pop round and talk him through it" I said. *"I haven't got the software anymore plus I don't do the client face to face stuff, I wouldn't know what to say, that's your job"* she replied. *"Don't be daft, I can post out a disc with the new software on it and I can handle everything from head office, you'll simply be in his area, a sort of area manager"* what a great idea I'd just had and we sat down and spent the rest of the day sorting out the Harrogate office and how I was going to build it up with Jane running it from the front.

I phoned the new client and told him about Beans Accounting and how my regional manager would be looking after him, I explained that Beans Accounting was a part of Hammond & Co. and he was happy with it.

I marketed around the area and supplied all the stationary needed, price list and head office support so that the Harrogate side of the business could build up, and it did. So much so that we put together an operations manual so that the business could be duplicated by someone else and still retain the same standards throughout, minus the toilet inspections.

Word got out that I had branched out and I received an email from someone in the City of London who was interested in a franchise. I hadn't put together any sort of franchise model, all we had was a manual and paperwork. We talked for a while and it came out that he didn't have any accounting or bookkeeping qualifications but wanted to promote Beans Accounting to his clients, I agreed and went away to think about how we could get around him not doing any of the accounting.

I talked to Darren about it, he was good at problem solving and was currently helping new businesses and the Chamber of Commerce by advising new start-ups how to be successful. After a few days of scribbling and bouncing ideas off of each other we came up with the idea that everything can be handled by the head office to keep everything to a high standard and uniform, and the bloke in London can get the work, be the face of Beans Accounting in the City of London, speak to the clients down there and keep them happy. All we had to do was get the paperwork from the client and deliver it back done, plus send the invoice. In return we'd give the London office a residual commission every time the client used us. This would allow the London office the chance to build a client base as big as they wanted without the need to do the work themselves, this way it would also free up their time to build the practice down there without worry that they needed to get the work done.

All we had to do was rewrite the manual and make some adjustments.

I phoned London and put the proposition to him which of course went down great because it meant that he could make money from our services. Rather than post everything down to London we made a trip of it, we went down for the weekend, stayed in a top class hotel on the South Bank of the Thames and made sure that the London office integrated with us in Wakefield and that everything was uniform and to my standard.

The *"Become part of an accounting practice where you don't have to do any of the work"* was rolled out and we duplicated the system to another 26 areas throughout the UK, each office being run by an independent area manager under our Beans Accounting flag, each office sending over the accounting work to the head office in Wakefield and being sent directly to the client from here. In return the area manager received a residual income throughout the entire client-accountant relationship leaving plenty of time for the area manager to promote his area and build his or her client base.

I have people who leave the business from time to time due to one thing or another, but I'm never short of someone to step in to their shoes, we now have a waiting list of people in areas who want to buy in and become part of the Beans Accounting practice.

POSH SHOPS & DRAG KINGS

For the first couple of years Hammond & Co. dealt with the smaller client, the plumbers, electricians and one man operations. We'd had a few larger businesses join us and even larger businesses were starting to use us. I had an array of different clients now and they ranged from the very rich to the very odd.

To show how different my clients can be, we'd had two email enquiries via the website, one from a jewellers and someone claiming to be a "private members club", the jewellers was a famous high street chain but a prestigious one, I'm not allowed to mention any names due to data protection and client confidentiality, but they have a branch in London and they're well known for selling the more expensive watches such as Rolex and Tag Heuer.

The very rich… If there's one thing I'm an expert on its designer watches and handbags, so I took the jewellers enquiry myself and arranged the meeting. I wanted to know why they were changing accountants and why they didn't have someone in-house doing their books. I travelled to their head office for the meeting where I found out that they outsourced everything including payroll. I upsold our payroll service and they became a client.

We'd been servicing the client for six months and I was invited in for a coffee and a catch-up by the managing director who was visiting one of their outlets in Leeds which had just opened in Trinity Walk. I combined the meeting with a shopping day and that afternoon I went into the new jewellers' outlet.

I walked in and before I could even get through the door I was met by a young lady who had too much foundation and not enough face to spread it all on, plus for some reason she'd forgotten to make her neck the same colour so her face looked like it was superimposed.

"Can I help you?, have you seen anything you like?" she asked in more of a painful drone than a question. *"I've seen lots I like, but I'm not here to buy"* I said. *"oh, well what are you here for, it's a shop not a library, have you tried H. Samuals, they have plenty to look at"* she said before looking at her colleague and smirking. *"I beg your pardon?"* I asked. *"There's a cheaper jewellers further down, they'll have what you're looking for"* I could not believe that this skinny over make-up wearing girl was talking to me like this, my blood started to boil and I could feel myself getting warm *"how dare you speak to me like that, you work here and just because you work here doesn't mean that you can afford any of the stuff you sell"* she just looked at me *"Plus"* I replied *"you have no idea how much money I have, for all you know I could be a rich business woman who's here to have a coffee with your boss"*, she stared at me and said *"I doubt that very much sweetheart"* she then started laughing with her work mate.

I was angry beyond words and I was more than happy at that point to get on the phone and have all the jewellers accounts dumped in a bin liner and hand delivered to London. I turned to walk out and bumped into the owner of the chain who had just walked in. *"Hello Dawn, you looked a bit pissed"* he said, *"well come to mention it, this girl here"* I pointed to her, at this point the smile had instantly gone from her face and her colleague was pretending to look busy, I carried on *"she told me I couldn't afford to buy anything from this shop and told me to go to H. Samuels, she also laughed at me when I mentioned that I might know her boss"*, *"Did she indeed?"* he said as he looked at her and she instantly went from an orange false tan colour to a bright red. He walked over to her and said *"This is Miss Hammond, she's a very good friend of mine and when she comes into this shop she's to be treated like a VIP, and as for not being able to afford anything in this shop she could probably buy the shop if she felt inclined"* I could now feel myself going slightly reddish, *"Do I make myself clear or do I need to ask Miss Hammond to ask one of her members of staff to arrange a P45 for you?"* he added. The skinny girl went quiet and we walked out of the shop, *"Fancy some sushi?"* I asked and we headed to YO! Sushi for a bite to eat.

The very odd…. The "private members club" appointment came around and I went to it with an open mind. It was based in Leeds just on the outskirts of town but situated within easy walking distance of the legal bit where all the Solicitors and Barristers hung out.

I walked up to the property which didn't look like a club in any way and saw a doorbell with CCTV camera in it. I pressed a buzzer, waited a second or two and a voice came over the speaker *"Hello, how can I help you?"* it said. *"I'm Dawn from Hammond & Co, I'm here to speak to you about your accounts"*, the door buzzed and the speaker said *"Come in"*

I went through the large heavy door and was instantly hit by the smell of perfume, an odd smell for a private club I thought, but didn't think any more about it and walked down a hallway where I was greeted by a tall man in a suit. *"Good afternoon"* he said and we shook hands. They were very soft and I noticed he spoke softly, he also has a womanly look about him, as I looked again I saw that it actually was a woman but she was dressed and acting like a man. I made light conversation for a couple of minutes, I mentioned the weather, the amount of people in the middle of Leeds but all the while I was trying to think of what they called a woman who dresses as a man, was it a drag king?, all I could think of was a reverse transvestite!

"So, about your accounts, what sort of club is this" I asked, because I sure couldn't hear any music yet. *"It's a dress club for private members"* he or she said, I was a little amazed that they had this sort of thing. *"I'll show you around so you get a feel for the business, can I get you a drink?* I declined and looked into one of the room where I saw a man as butch as they come trying a blonde wig on while a woman held out a large dress against him.

We walked further down the hallway and I looked in another room, this time a man dressed as a woman was looking in a big mirror and posing in a pair of red high heeled boots. I'd seen this sort of thing on TV and in magazines, but I never thought they were real. *"Here everyone can be who they want and feel safe, in return they pay a small subscription, and that's why I need an accountant"* said the man woman *"also, I need to know what I can and can't claim for"* she added. *"No problem, but I'll need some details, can we sit down and get things sorted?"* I said. We went into a room that was set out like an office but looked a bit like a dressing room with a large mirror on the dressing table that had makeup lights around it, very Hollywood looking.

I made a start on the paperwork and there was a knock on the office door, *"come in"* she said, and in walked a man dressed like a Las Vegas show girl *"What do you think of it, too much?"* he said to the owner of the club, *"Not at all, it's never too much"* she replied. I put my head down and carried on with the forms. *"Dawn?"* said the show girl, I looked up, it couldn't be me they were talking to, *"Dawn?, I thought it was you"* he said, *"Errr... Hello, do we know each other?"* I asked. *"I used to come into the shop that you worked at down at the market, you used to sell me false eyelashes and gave me advice on stockings"*, *"Oh! Yes, I remember, how are you?"*, he pulled a chair from the corner of the room and sat down beside me *"Well, that Birdcage place that I worked at, I'm not there anymore, I've been doing the caberet rounds"* I had no idea what he was talking about, *"What's the caberet rounds"* I asked. *"It's the gay clubs and gay bars, I'm a club turn, but what about you?.. I went in the shop and your mate said you'd just left and the last she heard you were trying to start a business"*, he moved a bit further and looked interested in what I was about to say as if it was a beefy story full of scandal, *"I left and started an accounting business, but that's about seven years ago now"* a big smile appeared on his face *"an accountant?, ooh look at you, do you do mates rates?"* he asked, *"I'm sure I could sort you out with a friends discount if you need my services"* his smile got bigger and he said *"not just me Dawny, all the club turns need an accountant coz we're all self-employed"*, *"I'm your man"* I said, *"Well you're in the right place if you want to be"* said Mr woman man the club owner.

I gave him a stack of business cards and he said he'd pass on my details, I signed up the club owner and gave a discount on the understanding that she'd pass my details on to her clients who may be in business.

That was almost two years ago and they have both been clients since, I've had a good few referrals from both of them but the most recent one, and the one who came as a shock was a Solicitor who telephoned us and asked if we could account for solicitors. Solicitors have to prepare their accounts according to Solicitors Accounting Rules, so you have to be qualified to do them. We took on the solicitor as a client and during a meeting he mentioned that he was friends with a certain woman who ran a private members club near his chambers in Leeds and she'd told him to come and see me about his accounting needs. *"Well we all need a good solicitor"* I said during the meeting, to which he replied *"and we all need a friendly environment to express our taste in fashion don't we?"*.

OPERATION MELLBOY

I don't really do accounting or bookkeeping for any of my family, I don't know why, I think that they just don't think I'm actually in business. I sit in Costa almost every day and spend time with my daughters and Darren and from the outside it probably looks like I don't have a job, let alone a business with 26 offices and its' still growing. I look on the internet for houses and we've seen one or two in London for a few million pounds that we'll buy one day, but from the outside we probably look like we can't afford a weekend in a caravan in Blackpool, and I'm sure that's what the family see, if they didn't they'd tell their friends about what I do.

I doubt very much that my family would even believe me if they thought that we could sort out, fight and rebel against the tax man. Go against the government and challenge them on taxation and legal matters and even go to court to fight them on behalf of clients.

Another thing we have to be good at is making sure that any receipts or business purchases are legitimate expenses and can be put through the books.

As I mentioned earlier, we have to bare client confidentiality in mind, so the following names have been changed to protect their identities…

The only exception to the family not using me is Mell *(not his real name as you've probably guessed!)*, he's married to my cousin Julia *(again, not her real name!)* and he runs his own business. Nothing's too much trouble for Mell, if you mention that you need the garden levelling he'll turn up the same week with a JCB and dig your garden up, he'll also take down the fence and gate at the side of the house to get the JCB into the rear garden.

You pop round to Mells house for a glass of wine and he'll open the full wine cellar, Darren goes round to talk business from time to time and he never comes home sober, five minutes with Mell turns into four hours, he's that type of bloke who you instantly warm to.

Which brings me back to fighting the taxman, Mell first asked for our advice when he had a bit of trouble with HMRC, nothing too drastic but it appears that they now have it in for him, I think in the last year he's been "looked into" three or four times, but his books are spot on and everything's ship shape, they just seem to keep picking on him. His VAT is always paid on time, his income tax is always paid early and he keeps his accounts up to date, but they still keep requesting copies of his records.

We've even gone so far as to alter his client file to resemble a James Bond 007 "Eyes Only" top secret file and labelled it "Operation Mellboy", but despite all this uproar from the taxman, Mell always takes it in his stride, other clients who have had a compliance check from the taxman have gone to pieces with the first letter, but Mell sends the taxman a Christmas card now as he reckons they know him better than his family do.

Whenever Mells books come in, we label it Operation Mellboy, we put everything to one side no matter what we're doing and prioritise his work. No client is more important than any other, but some are different, different in a good way, and Mell's different!

So why do we prioritise his accounts?.. is it because the taxman has a grudge against him?.. is it because he's family?... No, it's because we have to spend time taking out all the receipts that he can't claim for, but that's my fault, I said when he first came to me *"if you're not sure if you can claim for it, pop it in your receipts and if it shouldn't be there I'll pull it out, just write the reason you think it should be kept in on the back of the receipt"*

Sounds easy doesn't it?... we'll let's take a look at some of the receipts that have worked their way into his books that we've taken out, along with his reasons for it being there…

1 x Carbon Fibre Fishing Rod, Mell's reason it was needed: to reach hard to reach things that might fall behind something and I can't reach it.

1 x Fishing rod cover, Mells reason it was needed: to cover his hard to reach reaching device above and avoid damage to it.

1 x 70lb Carp fishing line, Mells reason it was needed: in case I have to reach quite far for something that's very heavy.

1 x Ford Transit gearbox, Mells reason for needing it: It was a cracking deal!

20 x Havana Cigars, Mells reason for needing them: I have 20 customers who are having babies!

1 x Ferry Ticket to France, Mells reason for needing it: I went to do a quote!

Mell's not on his own when it comes to receipts that we find in accounts, a couple of others from other clients consist of…

1 tub of weight gain protein powder, client reason: I don't take sandwiches to work and don't want to catch diabetes by not eating!

2 x Cinema tickets to see Saw 3 the movie, client reason: I'm a joiner and thought it might be educational!

2 x House Bricks bought from B&Q at 85p per brick, a valid item that could go through the books if the client was a builder, but this was a market trader who claimed: They stop my car rolling off until I can get the handbrake fixed!

Marks & Spencer Oak Smoked Salmon, client reason; I don't eat tuna since I watched a programme about Japanese fishermen.

We must pull hundreds of receipts out of clients paperwork that can't go through their books, but we always have to double check with the client to enquire as to its use to ensure that it's a legitimate business expense. But no matter how many receipts we see while putting clients books together, nothing is more entertaining than being part of "Operation Mellboy".

THE FUTURE OF HAMMOND & CO

Since starting out on the road that became Hammond & Co I have maintained a strict set of standards, Hammond & Co has since become the advisers to the prestigious client whereby I can charge hundreds or even thousands of pounds for advice or a couple of hours work. This is because I don't charge an hourly fee to Hammond & Co clients unless they are having bookkeeping done. I charge out through the value based system whereby my client gets the best possible advice and outcome in return for the fee paid to us. The clients that Hammond & Co. now attract are a far cry from the early days of builders and Netto bags full of invoices.

That said, we still service those original clients and treat them as if they are the only clients we have, my standards are echoed throughout the business and I am happy to say that every single client is treat the same, from a sole trader electrician to a national corporation, every client is important to me and unlike other accounting firms out there, we do not favour a client simply on their turnover.

Our Beans Accounting brand attracts a different client, one who knows what they want and again are happy to pay for the advice given. Beans Accounting has enabled me to take advantage of the market and has been a driving force for national coverage.

The market will always need Accountants and Bookkeepers, the government has seen to that, and so long as the red tape keeps getting thicker the businesses will need someone to cut through that tape for them.

So now you know my story and how a working class Yorkshire lass made good, you'll know that you can do it too. Don't you think it's time that you started your own story?

Being the enterprising person that I think I've become I'm always on the lookout for people who want to succeed in business, if you think you have what it takes to run your own area then please feel free to get in touch.

It's not free, but it's not expensive either and you can start as an introducer or you can take a full franchise.

Feel free to email me directly at:
dawn.hammond@hammondandco.co.uk

Or you can download a prospectus at
www.hammondandco.co.uk

If you want to go it alone then in the next part of the book you'll find a simple guide on how to start your own bookkeeping business.

Whatever you decide, just do it, don't waste time.

Good luck

D. Hammond

Dawn Hammond
Hammond & Co.

PART TWO

Disclaimer: The following information is for guidance only, please ensure you seek legal and/or financial advice before you embark on any business venture. What works for one person may not work for another and as such any information found within this publication should be researched prior to any action being taken.

SO YOU WANT TO START YOUR OWN BUSINESS?

Many people want to start their own business, they plan and plan and plan and plan until one day they put the plan to one side and don't bother taking it any further. You see, what you'll find with most people is that they love the ideal that goes with running their own business but they lack the motivation to actually do it.

They keep telling themselves that they'll start a business as soon as they can do this, or they'll start it as soon as they've learned that, and so on and so on until eventually the time has passed them by.

If you're an actor you practice and practice until you get the script right, in life we don't get the same chance. This is it, no dress rehearsal, just the adlib of life and no script. So if you want to succeed you have to do it, and do it now. If you're putting it off until you learn something then just put it off for ever and get a job, just quit and get back to doing what you really want to do and leave the business to those who actually want to succeed.

Now if you're still with me and you want to get started, lets' do it…

QUALIFICATIONS

I had to have some sort of qualification to start my business and I wanted to be in a position where I could show what I knew to the clients. At the same time I needed the money to pay for the course but I didn't have a client so I didn't have the money, a real life catch 22.

Qualifications can be achieved when your business is up and running, the main thing that the client wants when you're a smaller bookkeeper is someone to look after his or her books. You don't have to be great at it and I'd even go so far as saying you don't have to be good at it, you just have to be better at it than the people who'll become your clients.

If you can count, can organise and can put things in order, then input that information into bookkeeping software, then you can become a bookkeeper. It helps if you know what should go where and what invoice or receipt should be posted into what book (posted is a term used which really means written down in what section) but you can learn that as you go along.

The original course I did was meant to last 12 months, I can honestly say that the whole course could have been put in one book. Buy yourself a book about bookkeeping, there's one on the market called "Teach yourself bookkeeping and accounting in a week" so instead of going down the pub for a quick pint on a Saturday night or to that new wine bar that's just opened in town for a glass of wine with your mates, do yourself a favour and spend one week out of your whole life learning bookkeeping, you'll then be able to go out every single night when your business becomes successful and you'll look back and think "I'm glad I stayed in those nights"

Spend a tenner or so and get a good book, do the course later when you have a client or two and learn on the job, but be honest with your first client and tell them you're new.

If you don't have the courage to launch the business prior to qualifications or knowledge then you could use a family member or friend to practice on. They don't need to be in business, just pretend they are. Make a make believe business with them at the helm and practice your bookkeeping on them, practice your client care skills on them and have them give you feedback. You'll feel a bit of an idiot "playing" bookkeepers but keep in mind the big picture, one day when your practice grows you can repay them by talking about how they helped you out in the early days and you can repay them by giving than a drive around the town in your new Audi convertible.

SETTING UP

There's a few things you need to keep in mind if you want to run a bookkeeping practice, the first thing is money laundering and the money laundering regulations.

It's now an offence to operate an accounting or bookkeeping practice without being supervised under the Money Laundering Regulations (it's sometimes referred to as "MLR") and if you're not a member of a supervisory organisations such as the institute of certified bookkeepers or the AAT, to name but a couple, then you have to register with HMRC directly.

The cost at the moment (2013) is £110 and it lasts a year, you have to register with them directly and you can get more information on their website which is:

www.hmrc.gov.uk/mlr/getstarted/intro.htm

Each address that you work from will need to be registered at a cost of £110 per address, this means that should you work from home and an office then that's two fees totalling £220.

Next you're going to need to register under the data protection act. If you hold records then you'll need this, it costs £35 and you have to fill in a large application form, but to hold records you'll need it, information can be found at:

www.ico.org.uk

You're also going to need professional indemnity insurance, it's not a legal requirement at the moment but I'd hate to think that I didn't have it. Chances are that if you fail to cover yourself the first time you're not covered the brown stuff will hit the fan and you could be left with nothing. It's a dog eat dog country at the moment, everyone is suing everyone for no reason other than the man on the TV told them to or the dog on the crutches said it's good to sue people, and everyone seems to think that it's now the right thing to do. So get covered.

You don't have to be qualified to get insurance if you shop about on the internet and you stick to bookkeeping for now, but you need to be 100% honest, if you've no experience then don't say you've been trading for three years, be honest, otherwise should a claim arise and they investigate your knowledge they have the perfect get out clause.

HMRC agent reference numbers are required if you want to compile tax returns because as soon as you complete a tax return for someone whether paid or otherwise the tax man deems you as a "tax adviser". You can apply for some online via the HMRC website, but some have to be requested in writing, so visit HMRC and decide which services you want to be able to offer. If you're sticking to bookkeeping for a year or so then you won't have any need to get client authorisation so things will be simpler.

So let's recap… You've sorted the following out…

1. **You've registered for MLR with HMRC**
2. **You've registered for Data Protection with the ICO**
3. **You've got insurance**
4. **You've decided what you're going to offer and if you need to request an agent reference number from HMRC**

Easy so far!

WHERE ARE YOU GOING TO DO YOUR WORK?

You'll probably want to start with as little cost as possible so to keep the costs down you'll register your home as the place you'll be working from for the MLR certificate and registration.

Chances are it will be either your kitchen or dining room table, or you'll use a corner of your bedroom or spare room to work from.

You'll need to make it as office like as possible to give you the feeling of going to work and you'll need to have it as organised as you can so that things don't get on top of you.

It's really easy when working from home to forget you're at work and just get on with the day, flitting back and forwards to the work corner as you see fit. But please try to keep your work time professional, start at a certain time and finish at a certain time, even put a suit or dress on and get into the office mode. It will be hard especially when you may have children around your ankles, but it pays off in the long run and after a short time the family come to learn the new rules and it's not long before "mummies at work" kicks in.

You'll need a telephone, if you can run to a separate business line then go for it, but if your budgets a bit on the tight side then make do with the house phone but get a cheap answerphone to avoid any of the kids answering it before you can get to it. Leave a professional message on the machine saying that you can't take the call at the moment and you'll get right back to them, then if you can't take it due to noise from the kids or the dog' barking then phone back as soon as it's quiet. Sods law dictates that as soon as the phone rings the kids play up or the dog barks, so it's always better to miss the call, let them leave a message and get back to them rather than give a bad impression or worse still, the impression that you work from home part-time and your fees shouldn't be as high as someone who has an office, which is complete rubbish, but people are fickle!

Stationary is the next thing on the list, you'll need to put together a letterhead. The letterhead can also be adapted to make an invoice and thanks to the miracle of eBay and PC's you can now design your own using either the Microsoft stuff that's on your PC or by buying a cheap designing package from eBay. I've seen them go on eBay for as little as 99p and you can even get "Open Office" for free by using Google to find it.

Business cards can be bought from vistaprint, long gone are the days of expensive printing where you had to go to the printers with your idea, return a few days later to see the idea as a draft, then go the week after to pick up the printing and give him £100 for 250 full colour business cards. You can do everything from home now for a tenner. Your business cards are the first line of advertising when you meet someone new, so spend some time getting the cards right as they make the first impression.

Flyers: many people say that flyers or leaflets aren't a good idea as they give the wrong impression and any successful bookkeeper wouldn't need to use this sort of advertising. I think that the people who say this are complete idiots, they're missing a valuable form of cheap advertising that's targeted to the customers you want.

You can print out or photocopy as little an amount as you want and only use the amount you need without the need for waste, so you save money. The hit rate can be a bit on the small side, but you only need one client from this form of advertising and you're in business, also, you can print out one of the leaflets and pop it in a sandwich shop or chip shop and it gets seen by the people who want to use you.. the builders and other businesses.

I started out in this way and it worked out for me, you may get less clients that I got or you may get more, it really depends on your approach to leaflet dropping. One of our Beans Accounting offices use leaflets to attract new clients by targeting large houses on posh estates, the thinking behind it is that people who run businesses have to live somewhere, and it pays off with a constant trickle of new enquiries.

So don't be too quick to dismiss leaflet dropping, it works in a multitude of different ways and if you use my leaflet that I've enclosed in an appendix at the rear of the book, you should get a response.

So let's just recap... So far you've done everything regards registering with the government bodies that you need to register with to run your business legitimately, You've now:

1. **Decided where you're going to work from.**
2. **Been online and designed your new business cards and placed the order.**
3. **Designed your letterhead and invoice**
4. **Copied my leaflet and printed a few out to deliver in your local area.**

So what's next?

You'll need to be registered as self-employed and to do this you need to inform HMRC that you're working for yourself. You might only make a couple of quid at the end of the day, but if you make a single penny, if you buy something with the intention of reselling it, if you carry out any form of business with the intent of making a profit then you MUST register as self-employed as soon as possible.

If you look at eBay and the other online selling sites you'll see thousands of people selling items to make some money. It's perfectly legal to sell your old stuff if you don't want or need it anymore and keep the money, but if you look a little deeper you'll see that there are hundreds of sellers who are selling to make profit, selling things that they've bought to resell, and the taxman isn't told about it. How long do you think HMRC will stand for this?

At the time of writing, HMRC were putting together a number of tax task forces to combat tax evasion, online selling being one of the market sectors being targeted, how many people will they catch? And the worse thing about it is that once they catch you they can go back into your accounts years, they leave no stone unturned and they can even go as far back as the pocket money you were given in 1974 if they feel like it. Every month we are asked by at least one client to assist with a tax investigation, we have had so many requests that we now offer it as a service through our legal department.

So register NOW, it's easier to complete a self-assessment tax return than pay the price of non-compliance.

You're going to need a few bits and pieces to help run your business, one of the main things you'll need if you want to run your bookkeeping business with success is some sort of bookkeeping software. There's an abundance of different programs on the market, you'll have heard of some of the major ones such as: Sage, Intuits Quickbooks or even Kashbook, they all do the same sort of thing and you can do the same yourself with any excel based package.

A good place to start is eBay and I looked on eBay when I started and got a great deal by using an unbranded run of the mill program that did everything that Sage did, it just didn't have the fancy name associated with it. The client might want to go for Sage or a big brand, but it's up to you to prove to them that you can give them the same outcome and customer service no matter what you use to post their accounts into, after all, they're hiring you to sort their mess out, not the software.

Once you've printed out the accounts and presented them to the client they'll look just as good anyway, so start small and when you get more money then, and only then, look into buying one of the market leaders.

Paper, envelopes, pens, a stapler and calculator are also needed. You'll need plenty of A4 paper to print out your reports and staples to staple them together. You'll need a supply of C4 envelopes to put the reports into to give to the client and DL envelopes to send reminders and letters. The pens are self-explanatory and you'll need the calculator to double check figures and also, fingers crossed, to add up the hours to invoice the client.

So, the final recap before you start…

1. **You've given up a few days to read a book and learn about simple basic bookkeeping principles.**
2. **You've registered with the government organisations you need to register with.**
3. **You've got insured.**
4. **You've got business cards and letter heads.**
5. **You've got your stack of flyers printed out and ready to deliver.**
6. **You've registered as self-employed.**
7. **You've bought your accounting software from eBay (all being well its cost less than a fiver!)**
8. **You've got your supplies for the home office, and..**
9. **You've got your home office sorted out with the answerphone and a PC or lap top on your desk or kitchen table.**

So you're ready to go!…. You just need a client now….

A BIT ABOUT MARKETING

Marketing a home based bookkeeping business isn't as hard as it sounds and despite every college and university in the world running a course on marketing and making a big deal out of "the secrets of marketing" you'll be happy to know that there are no secrets to marketing. There's only hype created by a few who want to keep a mystical lid on the subject and make everyone think that there's some sort of secret that takes years to learn, well there isn't.

All you need to do to get clients is tell people what you do, tell your family, friends and everyone you meet. Give everyone a business card at every given opportunity.

Take your leaflets out and visit B&Q, pop a leaflet on every builders van that see. Put some leaflets up in sandwich shops, cafes, newsagents and chip shops.

Take a supply of leaflets and drop them through letter boxes of larger houses, shops and offices.

Before long you'll get your first client, it's just a matter of perseverance and the will power to keep going no matter what. Keep handing out those business cards and leaflets and letting everyone know what you do.

For the hard to get clients I use a two letter system, it's not cheap to set up so only do this when you have a bit more money and stick to the word of mouth and leaflets for now.

The two letter method starts where I make list of potential clients, I usually make a list of 50 as any more tends to get on top of me.

I then work my way down the list of potentials and phone them up to ask who it is that's responsible for the outsourcing of accounts, sometimes the person on the other end of the phone doesn't know what that means so I rephrase it and say *"Who does your company books"* they usually tell me the name of the person in charge at that point.

This then gives me a contact name and a person I can address the letter to. Don't skip this as it's a well proven fact that if you send a letter to the person who can sort things out, you have a better success rate and chances are they won't throw it away, unlike the person who opens the letter and sees no contact name on it.

All you need to do is copy out the letter on the next page and send it to the contact person at the company you've just looked into.

Letter 1

Dear Mr Smith

The Most Amazing Offer Available in the Bookkeeping Sector

I own a small prestigious bookkeeping company that specialises in your type of business.

Being a specialist in your business sector who best to trust with the everyday keeping of your books and accounts? Not only do we know your business sector inside out, I also want to offer you the most amazing offer you will ever see in the bookkeeping world.

We will compile your books and get your books in order and up to my personal high standard for your first months worth of accounts totally **FREE OF CHARGE.**

That's right, **AT NO COST TO YOU WHATEVER**, I even arrange for the books to be collected and returned to your place of work, office or home at **NO CHARGE.**

No other bookkeeper can offer this and combined with the fact that we are experts in your business sector, what do you have to lose?

If you would like to take advantage of this once only amazing offer then please feel free to call me directly on 12345 789098 where you will be given the utmost attention.

I look forward to hearing from you soon

Kind regards

A Bookkeeper
Proprietor – ABC Bookkeeping

PS. Due to the nature of this amazing offer, we are expecting to be inundated with replies, so don't miss out and take advantage **TODAY**

I wait two weeks from sending the letters and then send a second one out to anyone who hasn't replied. This time it's a little more to the point but stays friendly.

For the second letter you'll need to buy a couple of packets of aspirins from the pound shop, open the box and keep them in the blister pack found inside.

Cut the blister pack so the Aspirins are in twos, but so they're still in the blister packs and staple one to the top of the letter once it's printed out.

It will cost a little more to send this time due to the size, but you should get a response from the second letter from some of the ones who didn't reply to the first one.

The second letter can be found on the next page.

Affix Aspirins here!   **Letter 2**

Dear Mr Smith

As you'll see, I've attached a couple of aspirins to the top of this letter!

I've done this for one reason, as I didn't hear from you after sending the last letter to you offering you the most amazing offer available in the bookkeeping world, I thought you might still have a headache from doing your own books!

As well as offering the most amazing deal in the bookkeeping world, I also offer **FREE** collection and return of your completed books.

As I promise everyone who I meet in business the guarantee that I will remove their bookkeeping headache, I decided to keep my promise and send you a couple of Aspirins to help.

If you still have a bookkeeping headache and want to take advantage of the offer of a **FREE** first month worth of bookkeeping, please feel free to give me a call on 12334 567890 and we can have a friendly informal chat about your needs and how I can get rid of that headache!

I look forward to hearing from you soon

Kind regards

A Bookkeeper
Proprietor – ABC Bookkeeping

YOUR FIRST CLIENT

You've managed to get your first client and you'll need to sort their books out by posting things in the right place and transferring all those receipts and invoices into a nice crisp report, but before you do that you need to get things in order.

1. Make a note of the time you start work.
2. Make two piles, one for the ins (invoices) and one for the outs (receipts)
3. Once you've got your two piles you then need to break them down further by putting everything into monthly piles.
4. Then once you have your monthly piles you then put them into date order.
5. Once in date order you can open up your software and start inputting everything into the correct columns.
6. The software should add everything up or deduct everything for you and there should be an income and expenditure sheet that is to be used as the main page.
7. Print everything out with the income and expenditure sheet at the front.
8. Make a front sheet with the name of the client and the date of the accounts on and print it out.
9. Staple everything together and the accounts are done.
10. Now that all the ins and outs are in order, use paperclips or polly pockets to keep them together and have them ready to hand back to the client.
11. Make a note of the time you finished.

That's it, your first set of accounts are completed for the first client. You just need to make out an invoice and present it to the client with completed accounts.

SIMPLE CLIENT MANAGEMENT

You'll no doubt want to set up some form of client management system so that you can keep a record of when you did the books for them, how much it cost and when you were paid. The simplest method is a large envelope with the clients name on the front and any reference you use for them.

We use a computerised system with a filing cabinet back up and in the early days I used an envelope for each client until the practice got to the point as where I couldn't possibly handle the files. We eventually moved on to a bar coding system and now have an archiving system to store long term files and paperwork via an outside storage contractor. The envelope method works fine for as long as you can handle it, so keep the cost down for now and keep it simple.

Any information you have on the client, any instruction you take from them and anything you do should be written down and placed in the envelope for reference.

You can then pop the envelopes in alphabetical order in a draw or cheap filing cabinet.

THAT'S IT!

You have more information on the subject than I did when I started out, all you need to do is get on with it, it's easier than you think and once you get going you'll enjoy it too.

I've been in this game for almost 10 years now and I've never looked back. I've had a few patchy times like everyone else, but once you work for yourself and you become your own boss, you never want to go back to the 9-5 again... and the lifestyle that comes with your own business is worth working for too.

I wish you well in your business venture and it wouldn't be proper if I didn't offer the opportunity of joining me either as an introducer or as a franchisee running your own area under one of our brands, so if you decide you don't want to go it alone please feel free to email me at:

dawn.hammond@hammondandco.co.uk

Do you need an accountant that understands your business?

Whether you're a Plumber, Electrician, Joiner, Builder or other Tradesman, we know that you all have a number of things in common such as:

- *Demanding working conditions*
- *Unpredictable working hours*
- *No time for messing around with your accounts!*

The last thing you need to be worrying about when you're up a ladder is whether you've remembered to sort your paperwork out!

By choosing us to bring your books up to date you will be able to get back to doing what you do best..... Running your business!

We even come to your place of work, office or home to collect and return your accounts so that you don't have to waste your time.

Give us a call today on

0000 000000

Lightning Source UK Ltd.
Milton Keynes UK
UKOW04f2240080714

234819UK00001B/214/P